# DÖSTÄDNING

**Margareta Magnusson** was born in Gothenburg in Sweden. She has worked for many years as an artist and has had her work exhibited as far as Singapore and Hong Kong. She has death cleaned many times, for herself and others.

# DÖSTÄDNING

## THE GENTLE ART OF SWEDISH DEATH CLEANING

# Margareta Magnusson

CANONGATE

This paperback edition published in Great Britain in 2020 by Canongate Books

First published in Great Britain in 2017 by Canongate Books Ltd,
14 High Street, Edinburgh EH1 1TE

canongate.co.uk

1

*British Library Cataloguing-in-Publication Data*
A catalogue record for this book is available on
request from the British Library

ISBN 978 1 78689 110 5

Typ͏                                                    Ltd,

Printed                                                 S.p.A.

To my five children

'Putting your house in order, if you can do it, is one of the most comforting activitites, and the benefits of it are incalculable.'

Leonard Cohen

# *Contents*

## *Foreword*

The only thing we know for sure is that we will die one day. But before that we can try to do almost anything.

You have probably been given this little book by one of your children, or as a gift from someone in the same situation as you and me. Or perhaps you've picked up a copy for yourself, because it struck a chord. There is a reason for this. You have collected so much wonderful stuff in your life – stuff that your family and friends can't evaluate or take care of.

Let me help you to make your loved ones' memories of you affectionate, rather than upsetting.

M.M.

# Death Cleaning Is Not Sad

I am death cleaning, or as we call it in Swedish: *döstädning*. *Dö* is death and *städning* is cleaning. In Swedish it is a term that means removing unnecessary things and making your home nice and orderly when you think the time is coming closer for you to leave the planet.

It is so important that I have to tell you about it. Maybe I can also give you a few tips, since this is something that we will all have to face sooner or later. We really must if we want to save precious time for our loved ones after we are gone.

So what is death cleaning? For me it means going through all my belongings and deciding how to get rid of the things I do not want any more. Just look around you. Many of your things have probably been around for so long that you do not even see or value them any more.

I think the term *döstädning* is quite new, but not the act of *döstädning*. It is a word that is used when you or someone else does a good, thorough cleaning and gets rid of things to make life easier and less crowded. It does not necessarily have to do with your age or death, but often does. Sometimes you just realise that you can hardly close your drawers or barely shut your cupboard door. When that happens, it is definitely time to do something, even if you are only in your thirties. You could call that kind of cleaning *döstädning*, too, even if you may be many, many years away from dying.

I think women have always death cleaned, but women's work is not often in the spotlight and should be appreciated more. When it comes to death cleaning, in my generation and those older than me, women tend to clean up after their husbands first, and then they clean up before they themselves are no more. While one would usually say 'clean up *after* yourself', here we are dealing with the odd situation of cleaning up *before* ourselves . . . before we die.

Some people can't get their heads around death. And these people leave a mess after them. Did they think they were immortal?

Many adult children do not want to talk about death with their parents. They should not be afraid. We must all talk about death. If it's too difficult to address, then death cleaning can be a way to start the conversation in a less blunt fashion.

The other day, I told one of my sons that I was death cleaning and writing a book about it. He wondered if it was going to be a sad book and whether it made me sad to write it.

No, no, I said. It is not sad at all. Neither the cleaning nor the writing of the book.

Sometimes I feel a little uncomfortable with how unappreciative I am about some of the things I want to rid myself of. Some of these things have brought benefits to me. But I've discovered that it is rewarding to spend time with these objects one last time and then dispose of them. Each item has its own history, and remembering that history is often enjoyable. When I was younger, I never used to have the time to sit and think about what an object meant to me in my life, or where it came from, or when and how it came into my possession. The difference between death cleaning and just a big clean up is the amount of time they consume. Death cleaning is not about dusting or mopping up, it is about a permanent form of organisation that makes your everyday life run more smoothly.

Now, when I am not running around Stockholm, enjoying all that the city has to offer, I have time to enjoy all that my apartment has to offer, which is a reflection of my life.

The world is a stressful place. Floods, volcanic eruptions, earthquakes, fires and wars follow one another. To listen to the media or read newspapers makes me depressed. I would shrivel up if I could not combat the negativity of the world's news with good friends, experiences out in the natural world, music, beautiful things or just enjoying something as simple as a sunny day (which can be rare in our northern climate).

I would never ever want to write something sad; there is enough sadness out there already. So, I hope you will find the words and thoughts ahead helpful and entertaining, perhaps even humorous at times.

To do your own death cleaning can really be very hard. Maybe you have to downsize your home for some reason, maybe you have become single, or maybe you need to move to a nursing home. These situations tend to affect most of us at some point.

Going through all your old belongings, remembering when you used them last and hopefully saying goodbye to some of them is very difficult for many of us. People tend to hoard rather than throw away.

I have death cleaned so many times for others, I'll be damned if someone else has to death clean after me.

Once someone is gone, things can be chaotic enough anyway, I can tell you. There are many sad stories about siblings who start to quarrel because they want the same item. This type of situation does not need to happen; we can plan in advance to lessen the chances of these unhappy moments.

I had for example a lovely bracelet that my father gave to my mother a long time ago. It was given to me in my mother's will. The easiest way to avoid future complications among my children was to sell it! That was a very good idea, I think.

Later, discussing the sale with my children, they were fine with my decision. They had each been given something that had belonged to my father and mother. And after all, the bracelet was mine to do with as I pleased. Taking precious time to discuss one bracelet with my five children seemed unreasonable. Death cleaning is about saving such time.

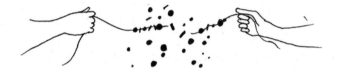

# Why I Am Writing This Book

I am now somewhere between eighty and a hundred years old. I take it as a responsibility of my old age to tell you about my experiences, because I believe this philosophy of death cleaning is important for all of us to know. It doesn't matter if it is your parents or friends and family who are getting older or if it is about time for you to begin death cleaning for yourself.

I have moved house seventeen times within my own country and abroad so I should know what I am talking about when it comes to deciding what to keep and what to throw away, whether you are moving house, moving country or moving to the Great Beyond!

Although it seems to be mostly women who death clean since they tend to live longer than their husbands or partners, sometimes, as with the family I grew up in, my father was left alone first.

If someone has lived in a home for many years where

children, grown-ups, relatives and guests have stayed and felt welcome, that same someone is often so busy that they never think of reducing the number of things in the household.

And so the number of possessions in the home grows quickly over the years. Suddenly the situation is out of control and the weight of all those things can begin to seem tiring.

Your exhaustion with all this stuff may appear out of the blue one day. When someone cancels a weekend visit or a dinner you feel grateful instead of disappointed, because you may be too tired to clean up for their visit. The problem is that you have too much stuff to deal with. It is time to change your way of living and it is never too late to start!

# *Precious Time and Helping Parents*

Today, of course, things are very different from when I was young. I did not say better. But the pace today is very fast. Many young families have to schedule their lives down to the smallest increment to have time to do what they consider most important.

Do not ever imagine that anyone will wish – or be able – to schedule time off to take care of what you didn't bother to take care of yourself. No matter how much they love you, don't leave this burden to them.

The first time I came across death cleaning was when I had to empty my parents' apartment after the death of my mother. My parents had been married for forty-six years and my father was not capable of taking care of everything himself when moving to a smaller apartment. Together we picked out the furniture, linen, household utensils, knick-knacks and paintings that would make his new home nice and comfortable.

My mother had been a very orderly, wise and realistic woman. She had been ill for some time, and I believe that she suspected that she did not have much time left and had therefore started to plan ahead for after her death.

As I began to clean up their home, I found messages attached to clothes and many other things: small handwritten instructions as to what should be done with everything. Some parcels were assigned to charity; some books were to be returned to their original owners. An old horse-riding outfit should go to the Museum of History, it said on a note fastened with a pin on one of the jacket lapels. There was also the name of whom I should contact at the museum.

Even if these small instructions were not addressed specifically to me, I felt consoled by them. I felt that my mother was there for me. She had really done some of her own death cleaning. I felt grateful, and it has proven to be a very good example for me of how to take responsibility for your things to make it easier on your loved ones after your death.

My five children were between one and eleven years old at the time so I was very busy. Because I had so little time, we decided to work with an auctioneer to clear out the house and to sell anything that my father did not want or need in his new, smaller home. An auctioneer may sound expensive and a little exclusive but it really isn't. The auctioneer's commission is deducted from the items that are sold, so it was no cash out of my pocket or my father's. Under the circumstances, it was the best option for us.

Auction houses are generally very helpful if you do not have friends or siblings to help you.

The auctioneer's office had to take care of a lot. I remember that as soon as they started it all went very quickly. I had to stop some of the movers carrying things down the stairs before the objects disappeared out of my sight for ever. But I didn't take it too much to heart if a few too many things went to the auctioneer's. I had so many things to take care of that were more urgent and complicated – such as my children's needs, my father's state of mind about the move, and our grief over the loss of his wife, my mother – that there was just no time to be too concerned with material things.

And besides, I had already made sure that my father had the basic things that he would need in his new home, such as household utensils and furniture. If a few too many things went to auction, it was not the end of the world. The most important objective was to hold on to the special things that my father wanted to have in his new apartment. We kept his beloved desk (where he placed a portrait of my mother), along with his favourite chair and a few paintings that he did not want to part with.

# How to Begin

Be aware of the fact that to downsize your home will take some time. Old people seem to think that time goes so quickly, but in fact it is we who have become slower. So, if you are in your later years do not wait too long . . .

This new job of yours will not be accomplished any faster if you wait, but with a little practice and preparation, it will certainly be easier for you to make decisions about how to get rid of things. Trust me, the more time you spend going through your belongings, the easier it will be for you to decide what to keep and what not to. The more you work at it, the less time-consuming it will become. You might even discover the added bonus that it will feel wonderful to visit a rubbish dump and throw worthless things as far as you are able to.

Start by checking the basement or the attic or the cupboards by your front door. These areas are great places to temporarily get rid of excess. Temporarily – well, many of the things you have in storage have probably been there for ages. You may even have forgotten what it is you have there. Good for you, because you will now realise that you will not miss anything if you throw it away.

Have a look in these storage areas and start pulling out what's hidden there. It may be a doll's house or ice-hockey equipment, mostly things that you yourself did not want around any more. Sometimes your attic has become so full that you are forced to put things in someone else's attic. Terrible! Who do you think will take care of that when you are no longer here?

Tell your loved ones and friends what you are up to. They might want to help you and even take things you don't need and also help you to move things that you cannot move on your own. You will see that a steady stream of people you like (or even dislike) will come to take things such as books, clothes and utensils.

Perhaps a grandchild or someone else you know is about to move into their first apartment. Invite them over, and you can show them your things and chat about them, tell them stories about the objects (or perhaps even your life) that they do not know. Meanwhile, have some bags and boxes at hand that you can fill while you are chatting, so they can take stuff with them right away.

## – *Pictures and Letters* –

Don't start with photographs – or letters and personal papers for that matter. It can be both a lot of fun and a bit sad to go through photographs and letters, but one thing is certain: if you start with them you will definitely get stuck down memory lane and you may never get around to cleaning anything else.

Pictures and letters that you have saved for some reason must wait until you have arranged the destinies for your furniture and other belongings. In general, when death cleaning, size really matters. Start with the large items in your home, and finish with the small. Photographs carry such a weight of emotion that they will hinder your work, but they are also very important, so I have given them their own chapter later on in this book.

## *What To Keep and What Not To*

The intention is not that we should remove things that make our lives pleasant and more comfortable. But if you can't keep track of your things, then you know that you have too much.

I feel comfortable in a home that is reasonably orderly. I don't want anything that my eyes do not like. If I have a beautiful chair I am not going to put my dirty laundry on it. There must be something wrong with the way I have organised my home if I have to continually mess up the place that I originally worked so hard to decorate and keep orderly.

Life will become more pleasant and comfortable if we get rid of some of the abundance.

# *Sort and Sort Out*

When you look at your home you probably see a bunch of objects that have only one thing in common: they belong to you. But in fact, most things you own have many things in common. Almost everything in our homes belongs to different categories, for example you can classify them as furniture, clothes, books, linen etc.

There are, of course, many different categories in different homes. Golfers, gardeners, sailors, football players – all have different inventories. Some of these categories are more difficult to handle when it comes to removing things from your home.

Choose a category that you believe is easy for you to handle. An easy category is one that is extensive and without too much sentimental connection. It is very important that your first choice is easy for you. I do not want you to give up immediately.

When you have managed to go through a couple of

categories you will feel good. Very soon your home will become so much easier to look after. I am sure that your family and friends will encourage you to carry on.

I always choose clothes as my first category. This is easy for me since I know that I have many garments in my wardrobe that I seldom or never use.

When I have death cleaned for other people, such as my parents, my husband or my mother-in-law, I always started with clothes. They are often so specific in size that unless you know a friend or loved one who is the same size, it is best to give all the clothes away.

But if you are starting with your own wardrobe, sort all your clothes into two piles (on your bed or on a table).

Pile 1 is for clothes you want to keep.

Pile 2 is for clothes you want to get rid of.

Then look through pile 1 and pull out items that require small adjustments or dry cleaning. The rest you can put back in the wardrobe.

Pile 2 is to throw or give away.

When I saw my piles of clothes I could not believe that I had bought them all. But I guess that birthday presents and Christmas gifts have added to the quantity. Some things are too small, some too big. If your figure has changed a lot over the last year I would add garments that no longer fit to pile 2.

Once I managed to reduce my wardrobe by two dresses, five scarves, one jacket and two pairs of shoes. A grandchild took a pair of shoes and the rest I gave to the Red Cross. Wonderful!

Our society more or less requires that we dress ourselves for different occasions. For everyday use, for festivities, for happiness, and for sorrow. We must also remember that our clothes help us to adjust ourselves to different seasons and work environments.

Perhaps you are among those who are lucky enough to have a so-called walk-in wardrobe, but if so, you will also be unlucky as you will have more clothing to air out, wash and take care of . . . and later dispose of.

When I was young, I read a great article on how to arrange a low-maintenance wardrobe. The point was that it is not the amount of clothing that makes a person well dressed. The article was all about choosing clothing carefully and then organising it well. I've actually lived with this advice for the rest of my life. Your wardrobe, as with everywhere else in your home, is all about organisation – so that you can quickly and easily find something suitable when you need it.

In my opinion, all garments in a wardrobe should look good together, and you should be able to mix and exchange them with each other.

Now, if you must reduce your wardrobe, it is good to take a few hours to go through it thoroughly to see what you can actually do without. There will certainly be impulse purchases and other things that do not really go with any other garments – when you look at your wardrobe as a whole, these are often easy to spot. Only keep those that you really feel you will wear, or if the sentimental connection is very strong. Sometimes a shock of colour or pattern against a simpler palette can indeed be refreshing to the eye, and a joy to wear.

I have a jacket that fits everywhere and nowhere. I bought it from a lady in a market in China many decades ago. It is a patchwork of many pieces of fabric and has embroidery representing funny fantasy animals. It is so colourful and carefully stitched together – a piece of joy made from recycled materials by someone imaginative. Was it the little lady in the market who made it? Maybe. I want to save this jacket because it makes me happy and I wear it on Christmas Eve.

But this is not a style manual . . . we must keep investigating, cleaning, organising and sorting!

# *More Organising*

It is always much easier to death clean a home when it is well organised. By 'organised', I mean that all things have a place of their own. When your home is a complete mess it is very hard to clean it at all. But it is never too late to do something about this messy problem. While you ponder where the thing you are holding in your hand belongs, perhaps you will find that you don't need it at all.

Where I live we have a club called Senior Net. It is a place where retired people, or actually anyone above the age of fifty-five with limited computer skills, can get help with their computer problems from retired and more capable elderly people. My helper was not happy with the disorder of my computer files. He looked at the screen and said: 'This is like putting your toilet in the kitchen.'

So he helped me. He organised my files. I was seventy-nine years old at the time, but I got the help I needed, and afterwards it was much easier for me to find my way through my computer.

The same can happen to you, in your home. You don't even need a computer to realise this. It's just a useful comparison, because in a computer everything is so logical and well organised.

# It Is No Fun to Play 'Hide the Key' When You Have Hidden It from Yourself

When my children were young we had birthday parties where we used to play a Swedish game called *gömma nyckeln*, or 'hide the key'. Oh, what fun it was! I would hide the key – a big old key from the seventeenth century – somewhere in our home and then let the kids loose. It was like hide-and-seek without some poor child having to hide in a cupboard and be forgotten. So, I would hide the key, and when any of the children came close to the little treasure I would shout, 'You're getting warmer!'

Too far from it, and I would say, 'You're getting colder!'

Such joy it was to play that game. But as an adult it is no fun at all when you wake up in the morning and cannot find your glasses. And no one says, You're getting warmer, when you look for them. Time to get organised!

In a home where you have been living for some time, it should be easy to keep some order. Still, I know families who live in a complete mess. (I won't mention the names of my children here, but you know who you are.) Mess is an unnecessary source of irritation. Even in a fairly small family certain members wander about trying to find their keys, gloves, certificates or mobiles. Whatever.

All of these things have something in common. They should, but don't yet, have a place of their own. Give everything a place and you won't feel angry, irritated or desperate when leaving the house. You will not find yourself standing by the front door so often yelling, 'Where are my whatevers?' And for a change – and as an added bonus – you may also arrive on time.

Most people clean their homes once a week. When you go through your home with the vacuum cleaner or mop, you will probably find things that belong somewhere else. Gloves on the piano, a hairbrush in the kitchen, a set of keys down the back of the sofa . . .

Carry a bag with you as you clean the house, or wear an apron with a huge pocket. Whenever you see something that is not where it should be, put it in the bag or the apron pocket. When you are finished, you can show everything you have collected to the people you live with and ask them to put their things back where they belong. Some households have so many misplaced items that a bag or an apron pocket isn't big enough. These households need immediate organisation. I have always organised my homes and cleared my clutter, so an apron with a pocket works for me. My apron is very stylish with a nice leopard pattern. In fact it is such a nice apron that I want to wear it all the time, even when I go out for dinner.

In a hallway it is always helpful to have hooks for keys on a wall and some baskets or boxes for gloves, hats and scarves. If you live in a house with several floors it saves time to place a basket on the landing of every floor for things that have to go up or down. But make sure never to put your foot in the basket.

Once, about ten years ago, I went on a sailing trip with a family for several days. Whenever everyone on board was ready to leave the boat for an hour or more, the cabin door needed to be locked, but no one could ever find the key from when we had last unlocked the door. Who had the key? Who had it the last time? Beautiful islands surrounded us, and yet every adventure off the boat began with a bad mood that affected us all and was always caused by the hunt for the key! Imagine how a little hook for the key on the inside of the cabin door could have brightened our lives on board.

Sometimes the smallest changes can have an amazing effect. If you find yourself repeatedly having the same problem, fix it!

A hook costs nothing.

## A Very Good Approach

The second time I came across death cleaning was when my mother-in-law died. She had already moved to a much smaller apartment and had managed to get rid of most of the things she did not have a use for any more. Her small apartment always looked beautiful, and it was nice and cosy.

My mother-in-law knew a woman who came to help with the things she could not manage to do herself. My mother-in-law called her Snow White. We never caught a glimpse of any dwarfs but Snow White possessed many of their hardworking qualities.

My children – her grandchildren, who were by then in their first small adult apartments – loved to visit their grandmother. She used to cook dinner for them and tell them about the time when she and their grandfather lived in Japan many years ago, when he had worked for the Swedish Match Company.

In the depths of the Depression, my mother-in-law and father-in-law and their son (my husband, born in 1932) had to return home to Sweden.

My mother-in-law was a highly capable and gifted woman. Returning from Japan to Sweden in the 1930s, she opened a small boutique in the city's main street. There she sold silk, china, beautiful lacquer work, baskets and other things imported from Japan. I believe she was the first Swedish person who used baskets for something other than laundry and picking mushrooms. For example she would use a basket for beautiful flower arrangements – a habit that is now very common and much used (you place a vase or any suitable container inside the basket so that you can pour some water in it for the flowers).

Very soon the upper-class city women would make their way to her shop, which she had called Mt Fuji. My mother-in-law had many pleasant – and unpleasant – stories about how she was treated by certain 'fine ladies' when she served them from behind the counter.

In the last years of her life, every time we visited her, or when she came to us, she would give us beautiful china plates, a pretty table cloth, or nicely coloured napkins to take home, pressing them into our hands as we left. That went on for many years before she made her last move to the small apartment that would be her final home. It was her way of death cleaning: over time she had slowly and unobtrusively given a lot away in a quiet, kind way. At the same time, she had added beautiful and useful things to her friends' and loved ones' homes.

At the time I never realised how thoughtful she was. Of course there were still things to take care of in spite of her thoughtfulness, but considerably fewer things than there might have been. Even today I feel grateful that she made it so much easier for us when she died.

# Happy People

I know many people who can sit in a messy home and look as if they are happy and in harmony. To me they seem almost comical. I don't understand them.

Yet I sometimes feel envious, as I myself cannot feel happy at all in a home that looks as if it has been tumble-dried.

When our gang of kids swelled to five in the space of only ten years we rearranged the main entrance of our home to resemble a Swedish primary school. Every child had his or her own colour, a cubby-hole in that colour and a clothes hook. All their outdoor clothes were hung on the hook, or put away in the little lockers. The kids' outdoor gear never entered the living area. To hang one's jacket on a hook and put the mittens in their place does not take much more time than throwing them on the floor. And the best thing is that the kids could find their things on their own, never having to ask, 'Mum, have you seen my . . . ?'

To hunt for misplaced things is never an effective use of your time.

In the case of death cleaning, disorganisation is also not a good use of your loved ones' time. They will not be happy people when they have to do your organising for you. So, work to keep things organised throughout your life and death cleaning will be easier for everyone.

# – *A Second Opinion* –

If you decide to downsize your home on your own, you may want to talk to someone about it, someone who isn't family and doesn't have a sentimental connection to the items you want to get rid of.

Maybe you want some advice or just other viewpoints from someone who is in a similar situation (other than me), or from someone younger. Preferably they will think differently from you, and that is good. It will help you to look at your work – or even other dilemmas – from fresh angles.

Ask these people to come over if you do not live too far from each other. Do not forget to write down a list of all the things you want their advice about. No one wants to wait around while you are searching for the questions you had in your mind. The following are some of the questions I have had when death cleaning:

Which charity is best to donate books to?

This painting has no real value but is very pretty. Will anyone want it?

Can I give an old samurai sword to my teenage grandson?

Not huge or difficult questions, but questions that could do with a second opinion.

# My Third Death Cleaning

The third time I undertook the challenge of death cleaning it was not in someone else's house, but my own. My husband of forty-eight years died after a long illness, and I was struggling to both clean up all of his things and to begin thinking of how to organise my own things for my move to a smaller living space.

When you have been a couple for many years it is hard to handle the fact that you have become single. My favourite oracle and problem solver was no longer around. He would never show up again to keep me company and to make life easier. This is a terrible fact that we each encounter in different ways, whether it is a spouse, or the inevitable loss of our closest friend or family members.

I tried to present myself as I believed others wanted to see me: that I was not going to break down and that I was working hard to move on. And yet, in a way, my dearest and best friend was still very present in our home, which made it hard to move on. I realised that I had to find a new home quickly, a place where there would be fewer memories and that would be more manageable for one person to look after – preferably without a big garden, or too many stairs and rooms to clean. I no longer enjoyed, or was capable of, mowing the lawn or shovelling snow . . . or interested in dusting, for that matter.

Compressing the contents of a roomy home with a spacious garden into a two-room apartment with a balcony is not done in a few hours. My grown-up children claimed some clothes, books, tools and furniture, but of course a lot of things remained to be taken care of, to sort, to keep, or to throw away.

I contacted an auction house, who looked at the things I wanted to get rid of and gave me an appraisal. Some of these things I put up for sale. I then asked friends and neighbours to come over and see if there was anything they wanted. After that, I went into each room and made a list of everything that was left in the room, and made a clear note of what to do with each item. Next to a lamp I would write 'Give to Peter', next to a painting 'Give to Aunt Ellen', next to something I couldn't place with a person I knew, I would write 'Give to charity'.

With all of this done, I allotted each room in my home one week to clear up. In this way I felt I could handle the death cleaning on my own, without rushing. Some spaces like the laundry room would not take a whole week of course, but there would be more time left to do other things around the house that would make leaving and selling it much easier. After each room was done I took a well-deserved break.

# Death Cleaning on Your Own

It would have been incredibly nice to have had my husband's company to help me get through emptying our home, my third death cleaning. But it was impossible. He was dead.

All my kids came home for the funeral, but the death cleaning took almost a year. I worked at a steady pace on my own. I kept in mind comments from my children about certain objects they adored and held on to those items, to give to them later, while cleaning out other things that no one cared about.

If I had asked my children and their spouses for assistance I am sure they would have done their utmost to help me. But I did not ask. Three of them had small children, and they had jobs in places such as the USA, Africa and Japan, far from my little house on the western coast of Sweden. It would have been too much to organise a visit from my children and their children and all their bags. Besides, I hate to ask for help.

To go through all the things that documented our life

together (fifty years of ups mostly, some downs, five kids) by myself made me feel very lonely. My husband and I should have done the job together, starting at sixty-five, maybe even earlier, when we were stronger and our health was better. But everyone thinks they will live for ever. Suddenly, my soulmate was gone.

In hindsight, I think that doing it on my own was probably a good thing. Perhaps it was easier for me to do it by myself. Had I cleaned with my husband, it would have taken us years. Men tend to save most things rather than throw them away. That goes for even the smallest nuts and bolts. They think, and rightly so sometimes, that every little thing will be useful at some later occasion. And had my kids shown up, they would have wanted to save everything. Everything! Or at least they would have had different, confusing opinions on what to save.

So, in the end the best thing really was to do the cleaning myself. On the other hand, if you have children who have huge amounts of time on their hands, by all means involve them in your cleaning.

# How to Discuss the Topic of Death Cleaning

When I was young, it was not really deemed polite to speak your mind to an older person, including your own parents. It was especially frowned upon for younger people to discuss topics that older people hadn't asked their opinion about first. To be outspoken and honest was regarded as impolite.

That is why adults at that time – my parents' generation and their parents before them – didn't have the faintest idea what young people thought about anything. The parents and children didn't understand each other as well as they might have. It was stupid, really, and sad, a missed opportunity for the different generations to know each other better. And death and preparing for death were not usually discussed.

Today we usually believe that honesty is more important than politeness. At best, we combine the two. I don't think that young people today are as 'tactful' and reserved as my generation was, and that can be a good thing for everyone.

Tact can be an important value so as not to hurt someone's feelings, but since we must all – one day or another – look death squarely in the face, perhaps tact does not have much place in the discussions we all must find a way to have.

Today we can more easily say to parents or anyone really: What are you going to do with all your things when you do not have the strength or the interest to take care of them any more?

Many adult children worry about the amount of possessions their parents have amassed through the years. They know that if their parents don't take care of their own stuff, they, the children, will have to do it for them.

If your parents are getting old and you don't know how to bring up the topic of what to do with all the stuff, I would suggest you pay them a visit, sit down, and ask some of the following questions in a gentle way:

'You have many nice things, so have you thought about what you want to do with it all later on?'

'Do you enjoy having all this stuff?'

'Could life be easier and less tiring if we got rid of some of this stuff that you have collected over the years?'

'Is there anything we can do together in a slow way so that there won't be too many things to handle later?'

Old people often have a problem with their balance. Rugs, stacks of books on the floor and odd items lying about the house can be safety hazards. Perhaps this can be a way to start your discussion. Ask about the carpets. Are they really safe?

Perhaps this is where 'tact' is still important, to ask these questions in as gentle and as caring a way as you can. It is possible that the first few times you ask, your parents may want to avoid the topic, or change the subject, but it is important to open the discussion. If you are unable to get them to talk with you, then leave them to think, and return a few weeks or a few months later and ask again, perhaps in a slightly different way.

Or ask them over the phone, or mention that there are certain things in their house that you would like to have and could you perhaps take them now? Maybe they will be relieved to get rid of a few things and that will help them to begin to see the promise and possible enjoyment of beginning to death clean for themselves.

If you are too scared to appear a little 'impolite' with your parents and you do not dare to raise the topic or ask them questions to help them think about how they want to handle their things, don't be surprised if you get stuck with it all later on! A loved one wishes to inherit nice things from you, but not *all* things from you.

## – *Did the Vikings Know the Real Secret of Death Cleaning?* –

Sometimes I think it must have been much easier to live and die at the time of our ancestors, the Vikings. When they buried their relatives they also buried many objects together with the body. This was to be sure that the dead would not miss anything in their new environment. It was also an assurance for the family members who remained that they would not become obsessed with spirits of the dead, from constantly being reminded of them by their possessions being all over the tent or mud hut. Very clever.

Can you imagine the same scenario today? With all the *skräp* (Swedish for junk) that people have now they would have to be buried in Olympic-sized swimming pools so that their stuff could go with them!

## Only Count the Happy Moments

There is a song that Anni-Frid Lyngstad from ABBA used to sing: 'Only count the happy moments, and forget the ones that cause you sorrow . . .' It is so important to make time for the happy moments that will become good memories later on.

Sweden has a very long coastline, and sailing is very popular in our country. In our family we used to sail and talk about sailing a lot. Very often our dinners would turn into veritable sailing races. Many pieces of cutlery were turned into boats in our imagination. Forks and spoons struck at each other, and the mustard pot became a rounding mark. It was a big fight to reach the finish line between the pepper mill and the salt shaker.

We talked about the latest race and we laughed about our shortcomings as sailors and later, remembering my husband, the kids' father, we cried as well.

When I was preparing to leave my house, I asked my grown-up kids if anyone wanted the table on which so many imaginary sailing races had taken place. All of them said no. Luckily, just as I was about to donate the table, one of my sons suddenly got a new apartment and needed a table, so there it is today. I am happy that this child will remember the happy races at that table and perhaps create new ones with his own loved ones.

Still, it would have been a nice table for someone else's home if a family member had not taken it. You can always hope and wait for someone to want something in your home, but you cannot wait for ever. Sometimes you just have to give cherished things away with the hope that they end up with someone who will create new memories of their own.

# The Little Optimist

A few years after our children left home, we still had a small wooden boat that we had used to teach them how to sail while they were growing up. The little boat wasn't in the way and we didn't really want to get rid of it, partly because it held so many fond sailing memories, and partly because we thought it would be a fun thing to have for a new generation should we have grandchildren. We wanted to keep the little boat around.

In our backyard there was a typically Swedish red barn with white doors and window trim. Under the barn's roof, the small boat found shelter to wait for those grandchildren. A wooden boat is sensitive to its environment; luckily the barn was neither too humid nor too dry, and so the boat waited patiently for a number of years, carefully looked after by the barn.

In the end, it turned out that none of the grandchildren thought sailing was especially fun and so we sold the boat.

We were sad. Though they were all sent to sailing school, most of them only enjoyed the lessons where they learned what to do when the boat capsizes and they had to survive in the water. That was a good lesson for them to learn, but the actual sailing part of the lessons never caught on or appealed to them.

The boat was a type called an Optimist dinghy. It is a beginner's boat. If that little boat had been able to speak, no one would have believed all the stories it could have told: tales of victory and defeat, tales of oceans and islands and fjords it had taken its occupants to.

I particularly remember a car trip to France for a sailing competition. We had our five children with us, a friend of theirs, and four little Optimist dinghies. One was on the roof of the car and three were on a trailer behind the car. When we reached Ghent in Belgium, it was dark out and we didn't know which route to take to reach our destination.

We saw a police officer on a motorcycle parked by the roadside. My husband stopped the car, rolled down the window, and asked for directions. The policeman looked at our load of sail boats and at all the curious little kids in the car. He blew his whistle and suddenly three more policemen on motorcycles turned up. With two motorcycles in front, and two behind us, we were escorted through town. Can you imagine how thrilled we were? None of this would have happened without that little boat (and its friends).

So, understandably, it was difficult for us to get rid of the boat. But what we learned from this is not to hang on to things that no one seems to want.

## – *A Woman's Job* –

I sometimes wonder how men cope when they become widowed. Men of my generation often manage poorly, especially if they had wives who spoiled them. They can barely boil an egg, let alone sew on a button. My husband could cope with most small daily things like simple cooking and mending. My father, who was a doctor, could clean the fish he caught very nicely; it almost looked as if he had operated on them. The fillets were guaranteed to be boneless! But could he cook them? Nope.

For a long time the best solution for widowers has been to get a new wife as quickly as possible – someone to do the laundry and ironing, and to save them from impending starvation.

I think that the next generation of men will be better able to cope if they are widowed. In Sweden, many young men enjoy both sewing and knitting, others are fantastic cooks and can combine flavours that make the mouth sing! And they are not so stupid as to waste time ironing the entire shirt when they intend to wear a sweater on top; they know that only collar and cuffs count. When these younger generations get old, their skills will be of great benefit to them.

I guess death cleaning has traditionally been a woman's job. Women have been in charge of the home and have also tended to live longer. We have often also been the ones who clean up after our children and our husbands, so we are used to cleaning.

Women of my generation were brought up to not be in the way, to not trouble their surroundings with their presence. That is not the case with men who take the space they are given for granted. My daughter sometimes says that I am so worried about being a nuisance that my worry itself becomes troublesome. Men don't think like I do, but they should. They, too, can be in the way.

# *Don't Forget Yourself*

While death cleaning you must not forget to take care of your present life: your home, maybe the garden, and yourself.

If you decide to downsize your home, it is a good thing not to be in a hurry. If possible, you should take your time and proceed at a pace that suits you. It will be absorbing but also tiring sometimes, and it is important that you don't overdo it.

When you remember the money you are saving by doing it yourself, and all the time you will save your family and friends who will not have to do it for you, it will really make you feel that the work you are doing is worth it.

Also, maybe you – as I did – will realise how many valuable things you have in your possession and that you want to let other people have them so that they can enjoy and take care of them. However, now is not the time to get stuck in memories. No, planning for your future is much more important. Look forward to a much easier and calmer life – you will love it!

Regard your cleaning as an ordinary, everyday job. And in between, enjoy yourself as much as possible with all the things you like to do. With friends and family, charity, walking, playing boules or cards. A friend of mine complained that it is no fun to play bridge when two of the gang of four have left the earth. That is of course sad. But young people are also nice to meet and play with, and they value your friendship as you value theirs. Besides, they do not talk about hearing aids and other depressing things all the time.

You will probably also need to use some of your time to see the optician, the dentist and your doctor for health check-ups and more. Those take time.

While death cleaning I have come to know some very interesting, funny and nice people when I have contacted auctioneers, antique dealers, second-hand shops and charity organisations.

Ageing is certainly not for weaklings. That is why you should not wait too long to start with your downsizing. Sooner or later you will get your own infirmities and then you'll appreciate being able to enjoy the things you can still manage to do without the burden of too many things to look after and too many messes to organise.

Sometimes I do miss my garden very much. But I must say it is much easier to just enjoy someone else's garden. (And if someone wants to learn or talk about gardening, they can ask you and listen: you still have the knowledge.)

# *Making the Move to a Smaller Space*

I read recently in an American newspaper of a whole new organisation of people who can be hired to help older people reduce their belongings and arrange their new, smaller spaces in the way they would like. I think it is a good idea, but when I saw what these people were charging, I worried at what the final bill would be: careful, thoughtful death cleaning takes many, many hours.

Hiring a specialist like this may also make the process go so fast – because you do not want to have to pay for too many hours! – that you do not get the peace of mind you need to really think over and plan your next home. Do not forget that you may live for many years to come. That is a good reason to go through your belongings carefully and ponder what furniture, textiles, books, paintings, lamps and so on you want to keep.

There are many ways to go about this. Maybe you have

a good model to work from; if not, here is my method to make downsizing as easy as possible.

I gave every room or space a name that I wrote on a piece of paper with columns labelled 'Give Away', 'Throw', 'Stay' and 'Move'. That helped me not to forget anything when different organisations (the old people's association, the Red Cross etc.) came to collect things.

When my house was sold, it turned out that the new owners wanted to buy and keep some of the furniture. I placed this furniture in the column 'Stay' and also stickered each piece with a label marked 'Stay' in red.

A little later I was able to find a two-room apartment in a different town that I knew well from an earlier time in my life, one in which two of my children lived and where I still had a few friends. I did not plan to pack, carry and move myself. Now it was time to get written estimates from at least two different removal companies, but before I decided on one I wanted to do more preparation.

# *Mapping out Your New Space*

Before I hired the removal company, I went to my new dwelling and carefully measured every space. The floor plan of an apartment that the selling agent provides you with seldom gives the exact measurements, and it is so important that they really are exact. Imagine that the furniture movers have carried a big chest of drawers up the stairs and it is five centimetres too wide. That would really be a waste of time and very annoying for both you and the movers.

So, first I bought a large pad of graph paper and outlined the floor plan of the apartment on it. I also measured all the furniture that I hoped would fit in my reduced space and drew them like squares and rectangles on a piece of the graph paper. I named them all so that I knew what they represented and then cut each of them out.

Then it was easy to furnish my new rooms by pushing around all the squares and rectangles of paper in the floor plan I had outlined. There was of course not room for all the paper furniture I had cut out, but the most important thing was to figure out which of the things I planned to bring actually had a chance to find a nice place in my new home.

Any items that didn't fit went through the same procedure as all the other things I had already got rid of. I asked my children first, then the auctioneer, then friends and neighbours and so on.

The day before the move I made sure for the last time that all the things that were going to stay were properly marked so that the movers didn't bring things I had already decided I did not need and that would not fit. This was as important as changing my postal address and switching my water meter and electricity bills to the new owner's name.

Moving into the new place was easy since I already knew where all the things would fit. I felt very happy and content that I did not have to ask for help later on to move things around once I had settled in.

# *Home*

I moved from the west coast of Sweden to Stockholm ten years ago. I made the right decision not to hurry when I moved out of my house. I took my time to plan my move and to really think over how I wanted my future to be.

This new apartment building has a lovely inner yard with a lot of greenery, trees and flowers. There is an outdoor seating area, a children's playground, bicycle stands, a garage for those who need one, a guest apartment that one can rent for a modest price for a couple of days, a well-equipped laundry room and good access to public transportation. It is important to look for the amenities that matter to you before you buy or rent a new place to live in.

I don't think I will ever move again, but since I am now between eighty and a hundred I do not think it will do any harm to make a new inventory of all that I have. I own too many clothes and too many books and I do not need sixteen plates when there is only room for six around my table. Also,

I am sure that the number of tablecloths and napkins can be reduced.

I have bought a small and easy-to-use paper shredder. I am looking forward to going through old letters and other papers that are no longer important – papers from a business my husband and I once ran, papers from other financial and banking transactions, and a lot of paid invoices with receipts attached with staples. If there is one thing I have learned from death cleaning it is that I hate staples.

My husband was very orderly, which was nice at the time, but today the staples are a problem. I have to remove these nasty little metal things one by one, so that they do not destroy my precious shredder. Tape would have made my life easier today. Keep this in mind when stapling papers together.

# A Few Thoughts on Accumulation and Other Things

I have spent my life painting pictures. Luckily, a big part of being an artist is being able to part with the stuff you paint. I have sold or given away my life's work, gradually, at the same pace that I produced it. When I had to downsize my lifestyle I had a number of paintings that I wasn't satisfied with. I had saved them because I wanted to improve them. In my new home there was no room for these paintings, so I got rid of them. I threw them on the fire.

Maybe the fact that I have got rid of my artwork all my life makes me unsentimental about getting rid of other things, too.

It is amazing, and also a little strange, how many things we accumulate in a lifetime.

## Things

New modern appliances such as deluxe coffee makers, high-speed mixers and sci-fi pots and pans fill our kitchens, while we still keep the old coffee brewer, whisk and skillets. In the bathroom you might have ten years of the latest eyeshadows, or all the nail polishes of past seasons. Medicine cabinets are often full of trendy vitamin supplements that

no one takes any more and medicines that have expired. Even tablecloths and bed linens have a fashion. We get new ones all the time even if the old ones are not yet worn out.

We feel like last year's colonial style of dark wood and bamboo has to be exchanged for this year's clean white Nordic minimalism, with straight lines and no fuss. If not, we seem to think that it is impossible to live in our homes. This is wasteful, but it's not a huge problem if we remember to get rid of last year's things before we buy the new ones.

This crazy consumption we are all part of will eventually destroy our planet – but it doesn't have to destroy the relationship you have with whomever you leave behind.

When you live in a big city where people seem to replace their kitchen and bathroom fixtures as often as I replace an old sweater, you will see huge skips on the pavements filled with bathtubs, sinks and toilets. When the next owner wants to put their personal stamp on the apartment everything is changed again – it may be in a year or two!

When you are between eighty and a hundred, you do not know many people your age who want or have the energy to do such large-scale renovations, or care about putting their stamp on things in this way. That is another benefit of death cleaning: thinking more about how to reuse, recycle and make your life simpler and a bit (or a lot) smaller. Living smaller is a relief.

## Clothes

When you get older, your lifestyle changes, as does your need for certain garments. I am sure you will gladly sell or give away gear that is more suitable for downhill skiing, ballet or perhaps scuba diving when you realise you are not likely to use them again.

I have gone skiing in a bikini on a wonderful, sunny winter day. It is strange to think that a swimsuit would work in the Alps, when ski boots most certainly don't work when swimming. So what do you keep when you get old? The swimsuit, of course.

People of all ages buy lots of outfits. Not because we need to, but because it makes us happy for a while. We feel better, more attractive, and we love the thought that the new outfit suits us perfectly!

Men my age do not really have the problem of too many outfits. They wear more of a uniform. But young men today seem more interested in clothing and fashion. So, eventually they, too, will have the same problems cleaning out their wardrobes as we women have today.

I have noticed that no one seems to mend anything these days, and the most expensive trousers are the ones that come with holes and patches. Perhaps it is time for new generations to learn how to sew and to fix things, as it would help our planet. Second-hand boutiques are popping up everywhere. I think it's wonderful! It's even called 'vintage' now. But what do you say when one of your guests shows up in your old dress? I really have to get used to that thought and have not yet figured out how to handle such a situation should it happen to me one day.

I was recently at a party with young people. A woman walked in with a very pretty dress. I complimented her on it and she was so proud that it was second-hand – almost as if it had been Dior. So, maybe society is changing. There is hope for the planet after all!

# – *A Note on Children's Clothes* –

When I was a child long ago, we had a seamstress as was the custom at that time. Her job was to resize and sometimes update my and my sister's clothes. Mrs Andersson arrived early in the morning to take our measurements before we went to school. She worked in our home for a few days each season.

I sewed a lot for my own children, and I have not forgotten all the trouser bottoms that I mended in the wintertime if they could not find some cardboard to sit on when sledging downhill.

Sometimes it is very hard to give away children's clothes. For me it is because they are so small and cute, and it is such fun to show a tiny shirt to a young man who is now almost two metres tall and say, 'This was yours.'

Later, when that two-metre-tall young man becomes a father, it can be nice for him to see his child in something that he once wore. The children's clothing of yesterday was of better quality than today. I remember how my mother made baby clothes for my children. She sewed them out of the same soft material that handkerchiefs are made of, and had all the seams on the outside so as not to scratch the baby's skin. I kept some of these items in a box in the attic, in case I was blessed with grandchildren. And when grandchildren failed to arrive, I would take the box down and remind my lazy children of what I wanted. It worked. I now have eight grandchildren. And no baby clothes in the attic.

But if smaller family members don't need them, the best thing is of course to give them to charity.

## Books

In our family we have always liked to read and keep books. A Christmas without a book for a present is a disappointment.

Books are generally hard to sell. I suggest that you let family and friends browse among the books you can live without and take what they want. Sometimes books have notes in the margins, written by people you know. These books can be difficult to get rid of for sentimental reasons. I suggest you give the book and notes one last read before you pass it on. When buying used books, I often look for volumes with notes in the margins written by strangers. It gives the book some extra character. So don't be afraid of giving away books with notes in them.

If you have several books on a specific subject such as, for example, art, gardening, cooking, science or, as I had, nautical books, you might find someone who is interested in buying the lot.

In addition to books to read and enjoy, most Swedish families kept an encyclopaedia set on the bookshelf. Nowadays with the internet I did not feel that I had a need or enough space for my encyclopaedias in my new apartment. So, when I moved from my house I called the nearby school and they were glad to take care of these twenty-eight (I think) big, heavy books. It made me so happy that I gave them a bookshelf as well.

I only keep books that I still haven't read or books that I keep returning to. In my case these are mostly books about art and some reference books such as a dictionary, a thesaurus and an atlas.

When I was death cleaning my house before my move, my greatest problem with my books were the Bibles. I called the local church but they did not want any more, not even old ones in leather bindings. They did not have any ideas for what I should do with them. I kept two – someone had written on the inside covers the birth and death dates of people from my and my husband's families who had lived long ago. The others I had to throw away. I do not know why I felt so bad about it. I guess that these Bibles had meant a lot to people who were in some way related to me, even if I had never met them. They were cherished at a time when books really meant something to the owners – long before Harry Potter and other bestsellers were invented.

Here in Stockholm the fourteenth of August is a big annual book sale. An entire street in the centre of the city is occupied by tables with books that people want to sell. It is a fantastic day for those who want to get rid of some books and for those who want to pick up more. If there is not something like this where you live, maybe you can help to start one.

# The Kitchen

One of my daughters has a sign in her kitchen that reads: 'I kiss better than I cook!' It is an informative and fair warning to her guests – that they might well have an evening of all sorts of surprises, perhaps both good and bad, ahead of them. I like to cook, although I'm certainly not a star chef, but I have collected many kitchen utensils during my life which I now must figure out what to do with.

When we lived in Asia, I bought utensils that were practical, beautiful and unlike anything I had seen before. Porcelain spoons, for example, so good to eat hot soup with, as one doesn't burn one's lips. A few large ladles made of coconut shells, great for soups, stews and salads. I also have a small tea strainer of plaited bamboo, far too brittle and beautiful for daily use, but so well crafted. After more than twenty years they still look just as pretty. These small things will be easy to place with anyone.

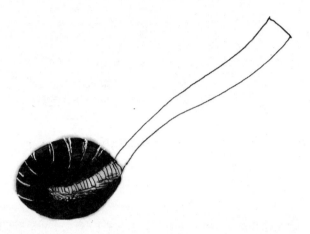

But I also had my big wok! Made of very thin sheet metal, black as sin, it is lovely to fry and boil with, especially when cooking Asian food. A wok like this must be handled like a baby, cleaned and dried thoroughly after each use, and sometimes, especially if the climate is humid, greased with a little oil so as not to rust.

Once I was invited to a tea party in Singapore. Everyone had to wear a hat – it was compulsory! I had not worn a hat for twenty years or so, and was not really well stocked in that area. I didn't know what to do.

And then I saw my wok hanging on a nail above our gas stove. I put it on my head, taped an orchid on the front as decoration, and tied it under my chin with coarse household string. Believe it or not, I won first prize and received a beautiful glass bottle of Schiaparelli perfume, Shocking, for my efforts. Wow!

A son and his family willingly took the wok off my hands. They love to cook and the food made in this wok, I imagine, has a special flavour. Moreover, they have a gas stove and also the option to use the wok as it is meant to be used, over an open fire, and in their case outdoors. Knowing that they had the right conditions to use this precious wok made it easy for me to place it with them. Thinking of the new home in which your object will find itself is very important as you do your job. Don't offer things that do not fit the recipient's taste or the space in which they live. It will be a burden to them, and if they think your feelings might be hurt, it may be difficult for them to say, 'No, thank you.'

If you are not selling something or giving it to charity, or throwing it away, careful thought in deciding on a new perfect home for it will satisfy both you and the recipient.

To know something will be well used and have a new home is a joy.

When death cleaning your serving utensils, there are two scenarios: either you are moving to a smaller home, in which case you need to consider the storage space available there, or you are staying put but have more plates, glasses, mugs, forks and so on than you can use.

If you still entertain guests, I would suggest keeping one set of dishes that match the amount of guests you can fit at your table. The same goes for knives, forks, glasses and cups. If you want to decorate your table use flowers or bright paper napkins instead of multiple plates and cloth napkins in every shade and colour.

I have kept, and still use, some special china plates from Japan, which I will give to my children. Simpler plates and surplus glasses have been given to charity.

## Cookbooks and Family Recipes

When my kitchen was larger than it is today, I had a bookshelf reserved for cookbooks. Nowadays I mostly use the internet when I search for a recipe. I type the name of the dish I want to cook into Google, and suddenly I get several possibilities, each with an image more alluring than the one before. Amazing!

These days I now have only two real cookbooks left. By

'real', I mean books you can hold, browse and pore over as you search for something to make. One of the books I more or less made myself over the years; it is full of recipes given to me by friends and relatives or cut out of newspapers. Most of these recipes I have been slowly throwing away: the time-consuming ones and ones for cakes and cookies. I no longer enjoy standing in the kitchen for hours, and I am not much of a cookie monster and don't really like them – though the children certainly loved them.

Some real gems remain, though, such as my mother's meatloaf, my mother-in-law's best *gaffelkakor* (a type of shortbread cookie topped with the imprint of a fork), my old neighbour Andréa's rosehip marmalade and a few more favourites that may be of interest to someone else, because they are so good, or because they are recipes that are not easy to find, or because they have resonant memories to them that my loved ones may want to conjure up in their own kitchens.

Three of the recipes I have saved are ones I found in my father's kitchen drawer many years ago. The recipes were handwritten neatly by the cook who lived with us when I was a small child. She was very kind, and I remember that I was allowed to sit in the kitchen and watch as she baked. She used to give me raisins as a treat, perhaps to keep me quiet, even if only for a moment. Her three recipes are for Pickles, Deep Fried Herring and French Steaks. Every other recipe she cooked was stored safely in her head.

The second cookbook I have saved comes from Singapore,

where we lived for six years and where I and many friends gathered recipes for a cookbook that we created and sold for charity. My tattered copy is full of delightful recipes donated by women – and one man – from all over the world. There is ceviche from South America, lamb curry from Malaysia, cake from the Swedish province of Värmland, and directions for how to make a perfect Singapore Sling. (Personally I think that drink tastes like someone cleaned out the pantry to find the ingredients – but I guess it fits in well with the wide-ranging tastes in the book!)

And there are cookies from Mexico, rye bread from the former Czechoslovakia and much more. Many of the recipe donors often hosted guests and were obviously very proud to offer something that represented their part of the world. Thus the amazing wealth of recipes. Browsing the book still takes me on a global tour of tastes and a wander through memories of the many fascinating people I knew at that time in my life.

When we came home again, to the Swedish coastal province of Bohuslän, where I am from, I thought about collecting old recipes that local women cherished and kept hidden somewhere – good things to cook that used local ingredients and recipes that may have been handed down, perhaps for generations. Now I do not think I have the time to do this, but maybe someone else who reads this will take the hint and get started. Now! Time is of the essence. These women might be even older than I am.

I find it has been easy to get rid of printed cookbooks, no matter how helpful they have been through the years. It is the personal recipes and stories that I most want to keep and continue to savour.

My next-door neighbour for a few years in Bohuslän was named Andréa. She was the very capable widow of a fisherman. She was a good, dear friend. I painted a picture of her once that represented a flowering dogwood tree. It is reminiscent of a magnolia tree but larger and covered with dense flowers. Strong and beautiful. Just as Andréa was. She had many wonderful recipes and a few I would like to share with you now: pickled rosehip marmalade, sherry made from red beets, and a classic cheesecake Bohuslän-style.

### Pickled Rosehip Marmalade

1 kg rosehip berries
600 ml water
150 ml white vinegar
500 grams sugar
5–10 cloves
1 cinnamon stick, crushed

Cut the berries in half and scoop out the insides with a small spoon. Heat water, vinegar, sugar and spices. When it comes to the boil add the well-cleaned berries and continue to boil until berries are soft. Strain out the cloves and crushed cinnamon stick. Pour into jars and close the lids. Does not have to be refrigerated.

### Red Beet Sherry

4 litres water
1 kg beetroots
2 kg sugar
250 grams raisins
100 grams yeast
2 slices of rye or other bread
(do not use white bread)

Boil the beets in the water until soft. Retain the water and pour it into a bowl. Add the sugar and raisins. Spread the yeast on the bread slices as you might butter a sandwich. Place the bread slices on top of the beet liquid. Cover and let stand for one month. Stir now and then (about once a week). Strain and pour into a bottle. Enjoy!

### Bohuslän Cheesecake

4 litres milk
600 ml double cream
400 ml buttermilk
8–10 eggs
50 grams sugar

Mix all the ingredients in a big saucepan. Heat it very slowly and stir from the bottom with a wooden spatula all the time. Do not let it boil. You have to watch the mixture carefully. When it becomes grainy put the saucepan aside and let it rest for five to ten minutes. Heat it up one more time, but do not boil!

Spoon the mixture into the mould or cake tin with a perforated spoon. The cheesecake mould or cake tin should have little holes in it so that excess liquid can drain off. Sprinkle some sugar between the layers of the mixture as you spoon it in. Or you can layer it in without adding sugar between the layers. Let it rest for about four hours.

Without sugar it is eaten together with pickled herring or smoked salmon. As dessert the cheesecake with the sugar is very good with blackberry jam.

One afternoon Andréa invited me over to sample her red beet sherry. It had a beautiful amber colour and tasted really smooth and warm and wonderful. That day she told me about the custom of fishermen's widows. She said that every morning, after her husband had died, she would take the leftover porridge and place it where his fishing boat had been moored. In no time at all a gull would fly in and dine on what she had provided. She said the bird was the spirit of her deceased husband. I always think of this when I see a seagull.

My own husband was buried on a glorious early summer day. The small girls, his grandchildren, were so serious in their bright dresses. The boys climbed up and balanced on a low cemetery wall. Someone read a poem by Frans G. Bengtsson, a Swedish author and poet whom my husband liked very much. The poem concludes that seagulls in flight know how to seek out places to rest; but the human heart, bound to life on earth, can never experience true peace while we are alive.

On the gravel path close to my husband's grave, a young seagull walked slowly past. I could not help but smile.

# Things, Things and More Things

Beautiful things such as an African wooden bird, strange things like a singing magnetic pig, and funny things like a solar-powered waving bear are all things that I adore. My vice is really things. It took me a while to understand this, but you can enjoy all these things without owning them. Even though this may sometimes seem quite hard to do, training yourself to enjoy only looking at things, instead of buying them, is very pleasing and also a good habit. You really *can't* take everything with you, so maybe it is better to try not to own it all.

All the things I mentioned above are small and easy to give away. If you are invited to lunch, don't buy the host flowers or a new present – give her one of your things.

When I browse through an interior design magazine I sometimes get so tired! Many of these homes look as if all the furniture has been supplied by the same shop. Colourless, plain, perfect, and without any charm at all. Too many pieces for decoration arranged on parade or in strange, affected compositions. Who will want to dust them, I wonder.

But there are many homes that have a lot to teach. Beautiful, practical and sparsely furnished. Truly inspiring homes that are easy to keep clean. I still try to learn from these rooms. I reflect and maybe rethink my own living space, and then probably will get rid of a few more things!

## If It Was Your Secret, Then
## Keep It That Way
## (or How to Death Clean Hidden,
## Dangerous and Secret Things)

In connection with my father's relocation there were a few things that worried him. He was a medical doctor and he kept all his patients' casebooks in his office. Of course he needed to get rid of them in a safe manner. Everything was written by hand or on his little Remington typewriter. Computers were not yet invented. Because of that it was easy to get rid of his files without a trace. We burned all the papers in an old oil drum at our country house.

Another problem was a parcel at the very back of his desk drawer. It contained a large piece of arsenic! It had been there for almost thirty years, since the time we were worried that the Germans would invade our country. Why my father had kept it there for so long was hard to understand. Maybe he had just forgotten it. Maybe he thought it would not hurt to have some poison available. The pharmacist looked a bit puzzled when I handed over the block of arsenic, but he took care of it.

While cleaning out my parents' house, one thing really puzzled me. My mother had a huge cabinet for linen. Freshly pressed towels and napkins were put at the bottom of the piles so that the rotation of all the items was even. At the very back, behind pleated pillow-case ribbons, I found her vice. Several packets of cigarettes.

What are vices? I guess habits that are not so good for us. We now become dependent on our mobiles, games and many other things that – unlike cigarette packets – do not reveal themselves after we are dead.

But there are people who have wardrobes filled with empty gin and whisky bottles that they have secretly finished off. And there are many other things that people love to gossip about after someone's death.

Maybe Grandfather had ladies' underwear in his drawer and maybe Grandma had a dildo in hers. But what does that matter now? They are no longer among us; if we liked them it really should be nothing for us to worry about. Let us each have our small preferences, as long as no one gets hurt.

But it is perhaps a thoughtful gift to those loved ones who may be death cleaning for us later if we do a little bit of our own cleaning now – to reduce those types of belongings a bit before we leave our present life.

So, save your favourite dildo but throw away the other fifteen!

There's no sense in keeping things that will shock or upset your family after you are gone.

Perhaps you have saved letters, documents or diaries that contain information or family stories you would never wish to embarrass your descendants with. While we seem to live in a culture where everyone thinks they have the right to every secret, I do not agree. If you think the secrets will cause your loved ones harm or unhappiness then make sure to destroy them. Make a bonfire or shove them into the hungry shredder.

## – *The Perils of Man Caves* –

Another space that seemed like it could be time-consuming to go through was my husband's tool shed. If you own a house, it is very convenient to have someone who also lives there who can be a combination of carpenter, painter, plumber and general repairer of things.

This can be especially so if you live far from a major city where all these professionals seem to locate their businesses. It can be very expensive if you need to call for technical assistance all the time if you live in an out-of-the-way place, as we did for many years.

Bicycles, boats and garden paraphernalia all need various tools and repairing to keep them functioning. There are endless reasons to justify the purchase of new tools, and men – or at least those in my generation and the generations before me – seem to jump at any chance to visit the hardware store!

But let's be truthful, you don't need to live in a house to have an overload of tools. One of my children, who lives in a small rented apartment in a city, has a cupboard full of odd nuts, bolts, screws, bent nails and fixtures that he thinks he might need one day. He hasn't opened that cupboard for years.

After all the children (who also need special tools: our children liked to build huts, rafts and tiny box carts – we call them *lådbil* in Sweden) left home my husband continued to organise and examine his many tools every day.

His *snickarbod* (Swedish for tool shed) gradually became what I believe today is called a man cave. In Swedish we also now sometimes call it *mansdagis* –

literally, a male nursery, which makes me smile and which feels like an entirely appropriate word.

Have you noticed that many people find more pleasure in organising their stuff than in actually using it? I have, and I admire that spirit of order immensely.

As I investigated my husband's *snickarbod* I saw that everything was beautifully in order: chisel, level, rotary hammers, pliers and hacksaw frames and lots of screws and nails! Pumps, and rubber valves, special oils for the bikes. It sounds almost erotic! The mower also needed special oils and grindstones, and the boat required all sorts of sandpaper, paint and other gadgets. All these things had been carefully and lovingly organised by my husband.

There were a few boxes marked with more loosely organised contents, but most of his tools were hung on the wall, matched to carefully drawn outlines to show where they belonged and as a reminder in case someone borrowed something and failed to return it to the right place. A master of order, my husband was.

If I had entertained any thoughts about becoming a craftsman, my husband's tool shed should have been an inspiration. I could have started sculpting in rock, iron, concrete, built wooden projects, connected engines for some unusual invention. Everything I could need was all there, with warranties and instructions beautifully organised in binders.

But these were not my ambitions and were not how I thought I would be spending my time. Instead I picked out one hammer, some pliers, a selection of screwdrivers and a yardstick for the small repairs and adjustments that I thought I could accomplish myself.

Hanging up paintings, shelves and putting up hooks for towels or garments isn't too difficult when you have the right tools. Even if you are very old. My children took some of the other tools, and their friends were happy to help clean out the rest as tools are relatively expensive in Sweden.

I found that it was especially efficient to invite young men over to choose things for themselves. They were starting their own man caves and my husband's *snickarbod* was empty in no time.

To empty the *snickarbod* was, in the end, fairly easy, both practically and emotionally. For me there was no connection to the items, apart from the fact that they had belonged to my husband. I had many other things of his that I felt more emotionally connected to. I never had to stop my cleaning to reminisce over an object and slow down my work. In the case of a man trying to death clean his tool shed . . . well, that could take years and I don't feel I have much knowledge to offer on how to do that.

## *Unwanted Gifts*

If you receive things you don't really want from your parents or someone else who wants to reduce the amount of their possessions in their home, you should be honest and say, 'No, thank you, I don't have room for this.' Just moving things someone does not want in their house to your house is not a good solution for anyone.

Or, you can do as I have done when I have received things that I did not really like. For a while I will put the object a little bit out of the way so that when the giver comes to visit they can see the object and feel happy about having given it a new home in my house. By the time I get bored of the object, I'll get rid of it – either to a charity, or to someone who admires it more than I do. But you never know, I have kept a few things that I did not originally like and they have become treasures to me; sometimes our tastes change and mature.

If I give a present to someone, I understand that it may

not stay with that person for ever. Do any of us really keep track of everything we give away? I don't. Things break. Even a popcorn machine does not work for eternity. I will never feel guilty for not keeping presents for ever. To be grateful and happy for a present when you first receive it is something different because that gratitude is not connected to the thing itself but to the giver.

I do know people who maintain what we in Sweden call a *fulskåp*, a cabinet for the ugly. A *fulskåp* is a cupboard full of gifts you can't stand to look at and which are impossible to re-gift. Usually these have come from distant aunts and uncles, and put on display when the giver comes to visit.

This is a bad idea. If aunts and uncles see their gifts on show, they will only give you more! And who can keep track of who gave what to whom and when? If you don't like something, get rid of it.

# Collections, Collectors and Hoarders

Have we not always collected things? Sticks and logs for the fire, berries and roots to eat? But collecting things just for fun is entirely different. I remember collecting shells on a beach on the western coast of Sweden where I was born. I still have some of them in a bowl together with some from more exotic places. Beautiful to look at, nice to hold in your hand. When I was a child we collected badges, bottle caps, matchboxes and pictures of football players and film stars. Also, I remember collecting the nice tissue paper that oranges were wrapped in when they were imported again after the war in the 1940s. We had not seen bananas or oranges for many, many years.

We also collected bookmarks that we traded with class-mates and other children during breaks. I had a very big and beautiful bookmark that I offered to a boy in my class if he kissed me. I think I did it to try to impress my best friend, who was four years older and was always bragging about how many boys had kissed her. But my appointed kisser never kissed me, so my lovely bookmark stayed with me and I think I was just as happy about that.

Later, I became more serious about collecting. Stamps became a quite lucrative and instructive hobby for those who made an effort.

I had an interesting neighbour many years ago. He used the basement of his villa as a shelter for all sorts of things. Flat tyres, a sledge, a playpen for children and other things. Over the years the room became quite full. The lady of the house discovered that there was a back door on the other side that led to the same space. Now and then she grabbed a few things and took them to the dump. When her husband wanted to squeeze in more stuff he consequently succeeded.

This summer I met a lady selling things at a local junk market. She and her husband were going to move, and when she went through the drawers in her kitchen she realised among other things that they had twelve cheese slicers. She was not a collector, just a bit careless. Then I read about a guy who collected egg cups. He was a real collector and had a thousand cups from different factories all over the world. Just egg cups. Amazing!

I had a beloved nanny, who collected coffee cups with saucers. She married a Lutheran priest and loved to offer church coffee in all her cups after Sunday mass in their parish. Sometimes large collections can be useful, but sometimes they can become a burden for you and later for your family.

If you want to get rid of a collection of your own, and your family doesn't seem to want it, I think the best way is to contact an auction house and listen to what they say. If they do not show any interest you might find a buyer on the internet.

A genuine collector enjoys collecting specific categories of things, has good systems for keeping track of the items in the collection, and looks for items that are missing in the collection. The collection will make other people happy, too. Think of museums. Are they not results of industrious collectors?

But people who just hoard things and papers without meaning or purpose may actually be affected by an illness discovered just recently. These people can fill rooms in their home with so many things that it becomes impossible to enter them at all. In some families and intimate relationships hoarding can become a serious problem. Unfortunately I do not have much helpful advice for you in this situation, but I do know that this hoarding disease can be treated. And if a doctor cannot help, the only thing I can think to do is to order a big container when the time comes.

# In the Garden

Most people have a hobby, something they like to do every day. Hopefully we are lucky enough to do it as a profession, but otherwise at least we can always do it in our spare time.

I loved the garden I had at my old house. For me it was joyous to go out into the greenery, to look and become absorbed. I would spend hours occupied by pruning, dividing, pulling weeds, replanting, or just being pleased by a plant that had recently opened a lovely flower. A garden is always full of adventure and expectation.

Later in the summertime I could fill a bowl with raspberries, give a sun-warmed tomato or a whole cucumber each to my grandchildren. These joyful moments will unfortunately disappear when you move up some floors, as I have.

When I still had my garden I had many tools to take care of it. I kept all my rakes and spades in my *redskapsbod* (Swedish for gardening shed). As I was moving to a place with no garden I let the tools in the shed stay with the new owners of our house. They were happy to have such good equipment, and I was glad to give it to people who were anxious to keep my garden pretty and alive.

If you are lucky enough to have a balcony, or even some window boxes, or a sunny windowsill, you can still have some perennials. I have an ivy plant and some honeysuckle, and they survive in their pots year after year without any winter cover even in this cold Nordic climate where last November we only had a few precious hours of direct sunlight. Every spring, when there is no longer a risk of night frost, I add some summer flowers such as petunias, forget-me-nots or violets and herbs like basil, thyme, chives and parsley to my tiny balcony garden.

In my apartment building, we have a garden group. The members take care of the vegetation in our yard. Everyone who loves gardening can get their fair share there.

In addition to green hedges and some flowering bushes, there are cherry trees that bloom so attractively in springtime and later on offer sweet berries. In the yard we have perennials that always have some plants in bloom. There is rhubarb and there are also herbs and spices like sage, thyme, rosemary, chives and lemon balm. Anyone from the garden group or from the building can pick some for cooking, or even just to smell.

The best thing about this kind of cooperative garden is that new members join every year. So, if one day you feel that you do not have the strength to work in the yard, the other members can take care of the vegetation and you do not have to feel bad about it. What could be better?

When I think of everything that grows and when I think of everything that we shred, tear and break to pieces and even bury to get rid of, it is a good thing that all that junk does not come back bigger and stronger the next year in the way that some plants and weeds do.

# Pets

And what do you do with your pets when you move from one home to another, or even from one country to another, or plan for your future?

Mice, guinea pigs, hamsters, cats, dogs, birds and fish were all animals that we kept over the years in our family. It sounds like a zoo, but we didn't have all of these creatures simultaneously.

Hampus, the hamster, belonged to one of my sons. When he was about eight years old, he let Hampus out of his cage and put him on our dining table, just when dinner was finishing. Grandma was visiting, and I had picked a large bouquet of goldenrod flowers which I'd placed in a vase in the middle of the table to brighten up the room.

Hampus approached the flowers carefully, sniffed them, and then proceeded to eat several of the blooms. Shortly thereafter and quite suddenly the little hamster gave a violent twitch, flipped onto his back and lay very still. Hampus was dead.

This was of course very sad. My son sobbed, looked at his grandmother and said, 'When you die, Grandmother, I will be as sad as I am now when Hampus has died.' His grandmother, being a very wise old woman, understood that he was honouring her with his somewhat shocking statement. She took him into her lap and let him stay there the whole evening, comforting him.

When we moved from the United States back to Sweden in the mid-1970s, we had to leave two of our dogs behind with two different families. At that time, there was a four-month quarantine for animals coming to Sweden from the US. Quarantine is a cold and lonely place, and something we did not wish for our tiny friends.

We thought a lot about how a little dog might respond when the safe home it has grown accustomed to is suddenly taken away and they must face a new environment, so we wanted to find a place that was just as safe. I contacted a kennel that bred Norfolk Terriers. It was not far from our house and was run by a nice middle-aged woman who said we were welcome to drop by.

The kennel was well maintained, clean and full of happy little doggies of different ages. The woman knew of our worries about having to place our dog Duffy with a new family. She walked us around the grounds and let us meet many dogs. Then we sat down for a chat.

While we chatted, a small doggy sat down very close to my son. The woman laughed and said to my boy, 'You see, that dog doesn't even know you, and he would still gladly go home with you!' We sighed with relief, felt reassured and were glad to have made the trip.

A secretary from the office where my husband worked took care of the little Norfolk Terrier, so he ended up in a good home where he was loved. I even got a comforting letter from Duffy's new mistress who told me that all was well.

Kennels usually have many contacts with people who are in a queue to buy a puppy or an older dog. Our Basset Hound also got a good home through the kennel. What a nice, funny and crazy dog he was. He loved to lie down in all the well-kept, pretty flowerbeds of the neighbourhood and to steal sandwiches and other edibles if given the opportunity. He had a good life with his new family, but as to the fate of their garden, I never found out.

Once you get used to having pets around, life can feel terribly empty without them. One day in Singapore, one of my sons and I set off to the SPCA (the Society for the Prevention of Cruelty to Animals), where all kinds of abandoned animals were taken care of by a full-time staff.

When we came home that afternoon it was in the company of a new family member: Taxes, a large, sandy-brown, old and rather tired Great Dane. Taxes soon made his home on a thick blanket on our terrace. He slept a lot, and most of the time slept so deeply that even though he looked fearsome, he was so kind-hearted that he once let some robbers step right over him without even trying to stop them when we were out of town.

Taxes was old with a greying beard; he was also rheumatic and could only eat a vegetarian diet of brown rice, mixed with egg and boiled vegetables. The mixture was so tasty I often caught my teenagers eating the dog food as a snack when they came home from school.

Despite these human competitors for his food, Taxes got a big bowl of vegetarian delight out on the balcony every afternoon. At every one of his mealtimes, two big black jackdaws would perch on the railing nearby to watch him. They sat there in silence, blinking their eyes and nodding their heads. Taxes always left a couple of morsels in the bowl. Then he went to his blanket to digest and immediately the jackdaws would come swooping down, land gently, and eat the leftovers. Every day! It was quite charming.

To own a dog is very rewarding but it is also a big responsibility. If you get sick or have to move and cannot take care of your beloved friend for a while, or permanently, you have to make sure that your good companion gets the best care and friendship possible. Most dogs are social and can easily make new human contacts, so they will enjoy their life without you. But with our dog Taxes it was different because he was so old and was often in physical pain.

When we had to go back to Sweden for good, I didn't

know what to do. I could not imagine leaving Taxes to an unknown fate. He was too sensitive to start anew and too old for me to find a family to take him in. I did not think he would be likely to survive the four months of cold quarantine it would take to get him to Sweden.

Finally, I consulted with our vet and made the only decision that I felt I could. It was painful and difficult to make. After they gave him the injection, Taxes sank quietly and heavily in my arms. It was so very sad, but it was the only option that we could see.

To let things, people and pets go when there is no better alternative is a lesson that has been very difficult for me to learn, and it is a lesson that life, as it goes further along, is teaching me more and more often.

If I were to have a pet now, when I am this old, I would

like that pet to be old, too. I am too lazy to raise a puppy, and can't go for the long walks a young dog requires. If I were to get a dog, and I think about doing this sometimes, I would go to a kennel and ask if they had an old and tired doggy that I could take care of. You could do the same, if your favourite pet dies, and you still want an animal companion.

Should your pet live longer than you, then you might be creating a problem for those around you. Talk to your family and neighbours before you get yourself an old lazy dog. Would they be willing to take care of the animal when you are not able to? If no, you should reconsider getting an animal at all.

# – *The Story of Klumpeduns* –

Is this a book about animals, you might be wondering. It is not. If it were, I would have to tell you all the crazy stories about our fish, our many birds and all our lovely cats: Mien, Little Cat, Little Fur, Shreds. But there is one cat I do want to tell you about: Klumpeduns (Swedish for a clumsy person).

One day, a big, light-red-coloured cat appeared in our home. My husband never had anything against cats, but he had never wished for one. Nevertheless, that red cat immediately adopted my husband and wanted to be close to him whenever he could. We named him Klumpeduns because he – unlike most cats – was always bumping into things and breaking them, leaping for things and missing them, or would just as suddenly fall off the chair he was sitting on.

Every night when the sports news was on TV and my husband sat enjoying it in his spacious armchair, Klumpeduns would come padding along, leap up and make himself comfortable on the arm of the chair.

Later, when my husband had to move to a nursing home, the cat mourned and missed him, but every night he would still jump up – if he didn't miss! – and lie on the arm of the chair, even though I seldom watched the sports news.

One day, the nursing home called and told me that my husband had suddenly died. I had visited him in the morning and, although he had been quite ill, it was still a shock. How could it not be? The nursing home asked if I could come and fetch his clothes and other belongings, as they needed the room immediately.

I had many other things to sort out once I got to the nursing home, but I brought everything from his room back to our home. I put all of his clothes in a pile just inside the front door, too tired to take care of it all just then. Some friends had invited me over to visit, and I really needed some companionship, so I left.

When I came home, Klumpeduns was lying stretched out and sad on the pile of my husband's clothes. I wept.

I had cried so much during the many years that my husband had been drifting away from me. That evening all my sorrows found their focus on that cat. I suddenly felt very guilty at having left the poor creature alone with his grief. Klumpeduns himself died a few months later.

Not that I really believe in an afterlife, but sometimes I find myself imagining that Klumpeduns has found a comfortable armrest and his good old friend in some other distant place.

# At Last: Photographs

I have come to my chapter on photos. These can be really hard to deal with – on many levels.

First, going through photographs is quite sentimental. So many memories come back, memories you will want to keep, maybe to give to your family. But remember, your memories and your family's are not always the same.

What one family member might think is worth saving, another might find completely uninteresting. If you have several children, do not ever believe that they will behave or think in the same way. No, not at all.

Even though we can all now save lots of photographs on our computers, I believe that most people still prefer to look at them in an album. While growing up, each of our children had an album of their own; since we took a lot of photographs it was always exciting when a new film was developed and the packet of photographs arrived through the letterbox. Every child decided which photos they wanted and put their name or a mark on the back of the photo so that we knew which ones to order copies for. Within a few days the photos arrived and were put into each child's album. They each still have their albums.

If you want to buy a nice album there are many kinds to choose from. I prefer albums with loose-leaf systems so that you can increase the number of pages as the album grows and time goes by.

Sure, it is nice to sit with someone like-minded and browse through a photo album. You can talk about when such and such event happened, compare your memories, and perhaps also remember the one who held the camera. It is like the back of the picture that you cannot see.

One of my daughters-in-law told me about a little girl in the nursery where she works. She wanted to draw her best friend. When the drawing was finished, the little girl turned it over and drew the back of her friend on the reverse side. What a wonderful idea!

So what should you keep in mind when cleaning out your photographs?

I usually discard multiple photos at once before I put them in an album simply because they are bad or because you or other people look completely crazy.

I have also always liked to be able to name everyone in a picture. Now that I am the oldest person in my family, if I don't know the names of the people in the photos, no one else in the family is likely to. More work for the shredder.

But sometimes I hesitate. Really old photos may well have a historical and cultural value even without knowing the names of the people in the photos: to look at the clothes, the cars and life in a street only thirty to forty years ago can be really fun. So maybe I should be a little cautious and show a few samples to my children to get a feel for what they think is interesting and whether it is something they would like me to save for them.

My father loved to take pictures and he was a very good photographer. I have taken many photos during the years, too, and three of the children are very talented photographers. As a result we have too many photos in our family, and it really is my fault. Therefore it is me who has to do the cleaning up. Me and my hungry shredder.

One problem with my photos was the huge amount of

slides that I have, all kept in cassettes. One cassette can hold up to eighty slides and I had many of them. We used to look at the slides projected on the wall. That was great entertainment since we had only one TV channel fifty years ago and children's programmes were rare. I think *Scooby Doo* was shown only once a week.

One autumn a couple of years ago I decided to do something about the slides. I bought a little film scanner and spent most of my spare time going through them: pictures from when my oldest son was born and the following twenty-five years.

With the help of the scanner I moved all the pictures I wanted to share to my computer and then exported them to a USB memory stick for each child. It is really amazing how much space a little memory stick – not even six centimetres long – can hold. I was happy to give them as Christmas presents that year. I just put them in envelopes and sent them through the post.

When you have lived a long life it is so easy to get lost among memories from a long time ago. It takes a lot of time, I know. It will be much nicer to go through old photos in peace and quiet later on after you have made some successful progress on other categories of objects and things. Plus, photos don't take up too much space and this is not a task your children will really resent being left to handle. They might even enjoy it.

I remember one time when all my grown-up children,

some with families, visited to celebrate a birthday. I had pulled together a lot of photos and sorted them into envelopes marked with the children's names. We were all gathered around our dinner table. At first, things were quiet as people opened their envelopes and began to look through their photos but after a while I heard them chatter: Wow! Look at you! Have you seen this! Do you remember that! And so it went on. It became a lot of fun. When everybody had seen enough, all the sorted photos were again unsorted in one big messy pile but I sorted them once more and put them in their envelopes to give to each child when they visited next. Some things are important to save.

By making games and events with family and friends out of the difficult job of death cleaning photographs you have gathered over a long life, it can be less lonely, less overwhelming and more fun. You also do not have to carry the weight of all those memories by yourself and you are less likely to get stuck in the past.

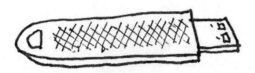

## Stuff You Can't Get Rid Of

There are things that are difficult, almost impossible, to throw away even when they seem useless and without value. For example, when I was about to move to my two-room apartment I discovered that I had forgotten a few family members who sat there looking at me with sad glass eyes. These were our most beloved toy animals.

No one had thought of them for a long time even though they had probably offered more joy and comfort than many human relatives. And I did not have small grandchildren to give them to any more.

One grown-up grandchild took a few for their own children – among them Teddyfer (a very strange name, like a fluffy Lucifer), a big white polar bear that I got from my husband for Christmas when living in Singapore and that I used to dance with when he was not at home. And Ferdinam, a big blue hippo with a handle on his back, a tassel on his tail and a striped beret on his head. I was glad that – like me – they were going to a new home, but I was sad to say goodbye.

Today, in my living room sits Dear Bumbal, a huge koala that my husband brought from Australia. I believe he had a seat of his own on the flight. He sits there and looks very content. On a shelf in my bedroom sits the Old Bear. He looks just like Winnie-the-Pooh. He is a bit worn and wears a sweater and socks to keep the stuffing inside his body. But he is actually eighty years old. He has heard many little children's secrets and been a comfort and offered companionship for many years. Shall I throw him in the rubbish? No way. He will sit on his shelf with a few small friends for the time being.

# The Throw Away Box

There are a few things that I would like to save for myself alone. Things that make me remember events that I may otherwise forget: old love letters, programmes, memories from travelling. I have gathered all these personal things in a box which I have marked 'Throw Away'.

As you go through your papers, maybe you will find letters in which the writer calls you wonderful things such as 'best and dearest friend', 'delightful' or other pleasant things that you want to read again and rather paper a wall with than throw away. When I find things like these, things that have absolutely no value to anyone else, but enormous value for me, I go and get my Throw Away box. Once I am gone, the box can be destroyed.

I know the first thing my children will do is check the contents of this box. But they can also choose not to. I have decided what others can throw away with a clear conscience, but I imagine that some of the letters, pictures and small things would amuse my dear ones if they did take a look before throwing the box away.

It is really very hard to do one's last cleaning. All the time I get stuck in different memories. At the same time it is nice in a way. I feel a certain relief when I decide to keep something small – a dried flower, a stone with a funny shape, or a beautiful little shell – and put it in the Throw Away box. The box is for small things that are just valuable to me as they remind me of special days and happenings.

It is very important that you do not choose a huge box for these items! A shoe box should do.

# Correspondence and Communication

In our family we have written lots and lots of letters. Mostly as a result of my husband's travels as a businessman for an international company. My mother-in-law used to complain: 'My son is like a satellite – he is always moving and often so far away!'

As our family moved many times to places far away from Sweden, we kept in touch with our relatives and friends at home with letters. Telephone calls at that time were very expensive, and only used for urgent messages. When the children grew older and visited friends, went on school trips, and later attended schools far away, they used to write cards or letters telling my husband and me what they were up to, or if they needed more money. I saved many of them.

Skype and FaceTime had not been invented yet so it took time and effort to keep in touch, especially from countries far away in Africa or Asia with poorly developed communication systems. We had to be content that at least letters did not travel by boat or with couriers on horseback; at least they could travel by plane so as to arrive sooner.

I really do not know if my grandchildren can write at all. I mean with pen on paper. No one seems to do that any more. I know that they are good at drawing, but considering the amount of thank-you letters I have received during recent years I am really not convinced that they even know how to write or if my present to them ever arrived. As such, Facebook is a good thing: through it I can see that a present has arrived and maybe even that it was liked.

When our kids were young they had to sit down and write thank-you notes. Considering the effort someone had gone to in order to buy and send a present, and then the joy of receiving something, I think everybody felt it was worth the trouble.

When a child is too young to read and write in their own language, and then has to move to another country where they have to learn a new language, writing is a difficult task. Our youngest wanted to write to her friends at home just like her older sister and brothers did. She worked so hard and I heard how she sighed. Suddenly she said, 'Mum, please write to them and say that I have died.' She was only six years old at the time, but perhaps already knew that dying is a way of being let off the hook.

Much later I visited Malta where a grandchild talked with his Scandinavian friends through his computer. For hours! Free! And they played games together. And they laughed! Could he even imagine how his parents longed for that kind of contact forty years earlier?

For my mother-in-law it was of course a terrible thing when her only child took his entire family to a country so far away that a weekend visit was out of the question.

So, once a week I wrote a letter to her, telling her about our life and especially what her grandchildren were up to. She put all these letters in a blue plastic bag and gave them back to me when we returned home. A whole family diary! I am so happy for that bag today. And I am not going to throw it away. If I have time I will make five copies of each letter instead, and give them to each of my five children.

In case I do not have time to copy all the letters, I have marked every envelope with what they contain and who it is about. Like skating on the neighbour's pool, building a playhouse from a wooden container or making a doll's house from a huge cardboard box, or parties, or making Christmas decorations.

## *Written Things*

I have some very old cards, invitations and letters. Some are more than two hundred years old. And they are so beautifully and carefully written, probably with that kind of pen that has to be dipped in ink all the time. Or maybe a goose feather, a quill I believe it is called. Written on very thin paper, now yellowed with age. They are really small pieces of art.

When I went to school it was very important to write clearly and neatly. Today not many people write diaries or letters by hand. And if they do, the writing is sometimes hard to read, especially for those who have never felt how a pen moves in your hand when a letter is formed.

We had a writing class in my school. Most of us found it extremely boring. The teacher pestered us to write with ink pens that we had to dip in inkwells often. One time we got so fed up with him that we poured water in all the small ink bottles. That did not make our writing easier to read!

I have no major trouble reading other people's handwriting, but young people find it almost impossible to decipher other people's writing styles. I guess that is why it is so hard for them to handwrite an answer in a letter. Of course it is much easier to sit down at the computer and click away something. It is fast and no envelope or postage is required. And you don't even have to walk to a postbox. But I still think that to receive a postcard in your postbox is happiness!

A young team of film-makers, including my daughter, is making a documentary on the great Swedish artist and film director Ingmar Bergman. They were having a hard time reading his diaries as they were handwritten in a style from almost a century ago, and so called on me for assistance. It was not very easy for me to decipher either, but it wasn't hell at least. Incidentally, I discovered that Ingmar Bergman thought about his death all the time, as is evident in some of his films, but didn't bother to do any death cleaning. In Stockholm we now have a huge Ingmar Bergman archive as a result. Perhaps sometimes it is not good to death clean – at least if you have made a great body of work.

I do not save the few and rare letters and cards I get any more. As soon as I have answered and thanked the writers for them they disappear into my shredder. Only if a card is extremely funny or beautiful will I tape it on the door in my kitchen, or sometimes I put it in my Throw Away box to revisit and enjoy again at a future moment.

# My Little Black Book

Sometimes I wonder if the next generation will be able to read small notes or lovely and interesting messages that they have received and will receive from relatives and friends during the years.

I know that there are many ways to save everything you want to save on your computer. I have friends who do not have access to the internet. They do not have a computer or an iPad or even a mobile and they have not bothered to do anything about it. Both men and women. This is very impractical. They say that they can manage well without this modern invention. Well, maybe so, but they are also depriving themselves of a lot of important information that could make their days easier and more interesting. Sometimes I have the feeling that I live in a different world to some of my friends.

I do not understand how I would manage without the internet. At least once a day I read and answer what has come into my inbox. It may be a simple question, an invitation or a regular letter and of course some advertising that I would like to delete. I might look for an address or a telephone number, pay my bills, buy tickets to a film or a train or air ticket when I want to go somewhere.

And if there are TV programmes that I did not have the opportunity to watch I can look at them on my computer at a time that is more convenient for me. You can buy almost anything. You can use it as a dictionary, as a cookbook and much more.

Technology advances so fast that it is sometimes hard to keep pace, especially for us elderly. Not only because we are slower than we used to be, but also because we forget things quickly and have to listen and learn all over again. This is of course very annoying and tiring. You have to write down many things. That is so very important when you use your computer. To enter certain websites you sometimes have to use a password. Over time the number of passwords you have swells and swells. They are too many to remember even for young people.

I have a small black book with a red back. In this little book I keep all my passwords so that I can access everything I want in my computer. And when the day comes, when I am somewhere else, my family can easily find what they need.

It is nice that the internet has made it easy to communicate, but in a way I think it is sad that so many written words and thoughts just disappear into the air. Who saves text messages on an old mobile phone? How many old phones would you have to keep in order to preserve some of your most precious texts? And all the chargers to all these phones if you want to read a message? Impossible. This is another problem with the advance of technology. All the gadgets that at one moment are a must, and the next moment completely useless.

I have tried to keep up with the times, and also do away with the old. When our eight-track cassettes from the 1970s became outdated, I threw them away. The same goes for my video tapes – I had them digitised and then threw them away. With my LPs it was different. A son-in-law collects vinyl and picked out a few that he wanted. The rest I threw away.

It goes without saying that I have also got rid of the outdated tape recorders and turntables that we played our music on.

While a beautiful art deco toaster from the 1920s can be pleasant to look at today, I think very few of our gadgets, chargers, routers and so on will be admired in the future.

# *Death Cleaning Is as Much (or More!) for You as for the People Who Come After*

I have already made the point that death cleaning is something you should do so that your children and other loved ones will not have to deal with all your stuff. While I think this motivation is a very important one, it is not the full story.

Death cleaning is also something you can do for yourself, for your own satisfaction. And if you start early, at say sixty-five, it won't seem like such a huge task when you, like me, are between eighty and a hundred.

One's own pleasure, and the chance to find meaning and memory, is the most important thing. It is a delight to go through things and remember their worth. And if you don't remember why a thing has meaning or why you kept it, it has no worth and it will be easier for you to part with.

These days I meet many relatively young people who do

not have children of their own. One might think: well, I have no children, therefore I need not death clean. Wrong. Someone will have to clean up after you. Whoever it may be will find it a burden.

Our planet is very small, it floats in a never-ending universe. It may perish under the weight of our consumerism – and eventually I fear that it will. If you have no children of your own, you should still be sure to death clean, both for the satisfaction it can bring you and for all the other children out there who you don't know. Recycling and donating can help the planet and also offer things to people who may need them.

One of my children who has no children of her own has a huge collection of books. This child (fifty by now) is desperately trying to find a young person who likes to read so that she can give away some of her books. Her collection is wonderful. She has always been a reader and many of the books from me and from my husband's parents have ended up in her library.

Most people will, if they look hard enough, find someone to give their things to. If you don't have children, you might have siblings, and siblings' children. Or you might have friends, work colleagues and neighbours who may be happy to receive your possessions.

If you cannot find anyone to give your possessions to, sell them and make a donation to charity. If you don't death clean and show people what is valuable, once you die there will be a big truck that takes all the wonderful things you have to an auction (at best) or a dump. No one will be happy about that . . . well, the auction house might be.

So, if you do not have children of your own you still have a duty to sort out your life. Go through your items, remember them, give them away. There is always a young person starting a new life, starting a new home, wanting to read everything written by W. Somerset Maugham (I admit this one is rare). You don't have to have a blood relative to give them pots and pans, chairs from your attic, an old carpet. When these young people can afford to purchase exactly what they want, they will pass on your old furniture to their friends, and then to their friends, and so on. You cannot know the places your objects may go after you are gone and that could be wonderful to contemplate.

If you give an old desk to a young person, create a story about it – not a lie of course – and tell them what kind of letters were written on it, what documents were signed, what types of thoughts were entertained around this desk. The story will grow as it is passed on from young person to younger person, to younger. An ordinary desk becomes extraordinary through time.

One of my friends was given a desk by a friend who was leaving Stockholm. It was from the turn of the eighteenth century. We look at this desk now. We sit and write at it, and always wonder what has been written on it. Who wrote sitting there hundreds of years ago? What were they writing?

Why were they writing it? And to whom? A love letter? A business deal? A confession?

It is a beautiful desk; we all appreciate this. But more than its beauty, it has been in use for three hundred years. I wish everyone who wrote on it had left a record. My friend has written a small note and tucked it inside. She will sell it soon. I hope the tradition carries on.

# The Story of One's Life

Death cleaning is certainly not just about things. If it was, it would not be so difficult.

Although our belongings can bring many memories to life, it becomes more difficult with photographs and written words.

They are all about feelings! Going through letters is very time-consuming – you will get stuck in old memories and perhaps dream yourself back to old times. It may be comforting and bring you happy memories but it may also move you in other ways, bringing up sad and even depressed feelings.

I have both laughed and cried reading through my old letters. Occasionally I regretted saving some of them. There were things I had forgotten and then suddenly it all came back. Again! But if you want to see the whole picture of your story and your life, even less funny things have to show up.

The more I have focused on my cleaning the braver I have become. I often ask myself: will anyone I know be happier if I save this? If after a moment of reflection I can honestly answer no, then off it goes into the hungry shredder again, which is always waiting for paper to chew. But before it goes into the shredder, I have had a moment to reflect on the event or feeling, good or bad, and to know that it has been a part of my story and of my life.

# *After Life*

It is hard for me to understand why most people find death so difficult to talk about. It is the only absolutely inevitable happening that we all have in our future.

How we would prefer to arrange things if we fall ill and how we want to be treated when we are dead are decisions that are within our power, if we face and take control of these inevitabilities. I know very well that we sometimes need professional help to go forward. Perhaps from a lawyer to draw up a will. But I am not qualified to give legal advice – I am just a death cleaner.

There are so many options about how we can think about and prepare for our own departure from life. No choice is wrong. Some wish to be cremated and have their ashes spread at sea; some want to be buried in a coffin. And of course there are many other things about one's death and funeral to think about. To spare your relatives and others from all these difficult decisions, you can actually decide it all by yourself while you are still able to do so. Talk to someone close about your wishes or write them down. Just try to be practical!

In this book I wanted to get you started with your cleaning and make you feel good when you think of all the hours you will have saved your loved ones because they will not have to use their precious time to take care of stuff you do not want yourself any more. I will feel so content and happy when I have done most of this work. Maybe I can still manage to travel somewhere, or buy myself flowers and invite some friends to a nice dinner to celebrate all the work done. And if I don't die I will probably go shopping. Again!

# *Acknowledgements*

I want to thank Stephen Morrison for inspiring me to write this book and giving me so much friendly advice along the way.

Also I would like to thank my publishers Nan Graham and Kara Watson at Scribner, Jamie Byng, Jenny Todd and Hannah Knowles at Canongate and Henry Rosenbloom at Scribe for their thoughtful input which made my book so much better. I also want to thank Susanna Lea for her hard work and for a wonderful lunch in Stockholm and to her incredible team Laura, Mark, Cece, Kerry and Lauren who have made this ride so pleasantly smooth.

And lastly I would like to thank my daughter Jane and her husband Lars. Without them this book would never have come about.

# *About the Author*

Photo credit: Jane Magnusson

I have been asked for my biography! Do I have one?

I know I was born in Gothenburg, Sweden, on New Year's Eve. That was good timing! As a child I thought that it was because of me that all the church bells rang, all the boats in the harbour blew their horns, and the fireworks crackled and sparkled in the sky.

My parents loved me, even when I screamed. My father was a doctor, and my mother stayed at home and organised the life they led. At that time it was very common for women to stay at home full-time, even though she had been educated as a nurse.

I went to a non-religious, co-ed school at age seven. After I graduated from secondary school, I was admitted to Beckman's College of Design in Stockholm. When I'd finished my education there, it was easy for me to get a job because the school was well regarded, but it was hard for me to choose what I wanted to do. I found work as a fashion and advertisement designer at a large department store that sold everything except food and stationery.

When the children started to arrive, I began working from home, delivering drawings while carrying a baby in a basket. I also painted a lot with oil and watercolours and ink. My first solo exhibition was in Gothenburg in 1979. Later I had more shows in Stockholm, Singapore and Hong Kong, and many other places in Sweden, too. When a painting in a gallery has been sold, it is the custom to put a circular red sticker on the wall next to it. At a number of these exhibitions, I sold so many paintings that we used to joke that the gallery had caught the measles. I enjoyed my career as an artist and still enjoy painting and drawing. I think I will keep my brushes, drawing papers and paints till the end.

I have had such fun, but now that I am aged somewhere

between eighty and a hundred I am getting a little tired and want to slow down. I have collected many things over the years, and it gives me such joy to go through them all. Sorting through everything is sad sometimes, too, but I really do not want to give my beloved children and their families too much trouble with my stuff after I am gone. That is why I want to tell others about death cleaning, and how wonderful and challenging it can be!

'Glorious'
*Telegraph*

'A gorgeous book'
*Good Housekeeping*

'A delight'
*Daily Express*

The Number One International Bestseller

# PENGUIN BLOOM

The odd little bird who saved a family

**Cameron Bloom
& Bradley Trevor Greive**

'Unique and remarkable'
NAOMI WATTS

CANON‖GATE

# REASONS TO STAY ALIVE

## Matt Haig

CANON❚GATE